NATURE designed a forest as an experiment in unpredictability; we are trying to design a regulated forest. Nature designed a forest over a landscape; we are trying to design a forest on each lecture. Nature designed a forest with diversity; we are trying to design a forest with simplistic uniformity. Nature designed a forest of interrelated processes; we are trying to design a forest based on isolated products. Nature designed a forest in which all elements are neutral; we are trying to design a forest in which we perceive some elements to be good and others bad. Nature designed a forest to be a flexible, timeless continuum of species; we are trying to design a forest to be a rigid, time-constrained monoculture. Nature designed a forest to be self-sustaining and self-repairing; we are designing a forest to require increasing external subsidies—fertilizers, herbicides, and pesticides. Nature designed forests of the Pacific Northwest to live 500 to 1,200 years; we are designing a forest that may live 100 years. Nature designed Pacific Northwest forests to be unique in the world, with twenty-five species of conifers, the longest lived and the largest of their genera anywhere; we are designing a forest that is largely a single-species on a short rotation. Everything we humans have been doing to the forest is an attempt to push nature to a higher sustained yield. We fail to recognize, however, that we must have a sustainable forest before we can have a sustainable yield (harvest). In other words, we cannot have a sustainable forest to have a sustainable yield until we have a sustainable forest. We must have a sustainable yield; we must have a sustainable yield to have a sustainable industry. We must have a sustainable industry to have a sustainable economy; we must have a sustainable economy to have a sustainable society.

Chris Maser

Lines from "Logging"

The ancient forests of China logged
    and the hills slipped into the Yellow Sea.
Squared beams, log dogs,
    on a tamped-earth still.
San Francisco 2 X 4s
    were the woods around Seattle:
Someone killed and someone built, a house,
    a forest, wrecked or raised
All America hung on a hook
    & burned by men, in their own praise.

Snow on fresh stumps and brush-piles.
The generator starts and rumbles
    in the frosty dawn
I wake from bitter dreams,
Rise and build a fire,
Pull on and lace the stiff cold boots
Eat huge flapjacks by a gloomy Swede
In splintery cookhouse light
    grab my tin pisspot hat
Ride off to the show in a crummy-truck
And start the Cat.

"Pines grasp the clouds with iron claws
like dragons rising from sleep"
250,000 board-feet a day
If both Cats keep working
& nobody gets hurt

—Gary Snyder

Copyright © 1993 The Foundation for Deep Ecology

All photographs copyright © 1993 the photographers as noted. All essays copyright © 1993 the writers as noted.

All rights reserved under International and Pan-American Copyright Conventions.

No part of this book may be reproduced in any form or by any electronic or mechanical means, including information storage and retrieval systems, without permission in writing from the publisher.

Clearcut : the tragedy of industrial forestry / edited by Bill Devall.

p.   cm.

Includes bibliographical references.

ISBN 0-87156-494-7

1. Clearcutting—Environmental aspects—United States.

2. Clearcutting—Environmental aspects—Canada.   3. Forest ecology—
United States.   4. Forest ecology—Canada. I.   Devall, Bill, 1938-.

SD387.C58C53   1994

33375´137´097—dc20   93-35989
                                                  CIP

Published by Sierra Club Books and Earth Island Press, San Francisco, California.

Design by Tamotsu Yagi/DelRae Roth.

Grateful acknowledgment is made to the following for permission to reprint copyrighted material:

Gordon Robinson, *The Forest and the Trees*, 1988, used with permission from
Island Press, Washington, D.C. and Covelo, California.

Random House, Inc. for permission to reprint an excerpt from the poem "The Tower Beyond Tragedy" by Robinson Jeffers
from *The Selected Poetry of Robinson Jeffers*. Copyright 1925 and renewed 1953 by Robinson Jeffers.
Reprinted by permission of Random House, Inc.

Cedric Wright, *Words of the Earth*, 1960, used with permission from the Sierra Club, San Francisco, California.

Portions of "Policy in the Woods" from *Ghost Bears*, 1992, by R. Edward Grumbine, used with permission of Island Press,
Washington, D.C. and Covelo, California.

"Escape" by D. H. Lawrence, from THE COMPLETE POEMS OF D. H. LAWRENCE by D. H. Lawrence, Edited by V. de Sola
Pinto & F. W. Roberts. Copyright © 1964, 1971 by Angelo Ravagli and C. M. Weekley, Executors of the Estate of Frieda Lawrence
Ravagli. Used by permission of Viking Penguin, a division of Penguin Books USA Inc.

Printed and bound in Japan.

DEDICATION

This book is in memory of the plantlife, birds, insects, animals, and indigenous cultures that have been driven to extinction by the greed and delusion of human arrogance. All of us in the Industrial Growth Society must take the responsibility for this condition and make it our duty to halt the continuation of economic and social structures that perpetuate this "death of birth."

We must try to visualize extinction and learn to understand accurately how certain patterns of human behavior lead to the extinction of species. We *do* have the ability to enrich, not impoverish, our lives and the planet wherein we dwell. We pray and hope for the continuing evolution of forest ecosystems. We work for realistic, ecological, sustainable interpenetration of humans and forest ecosystems, living by ecological terms rather than economic terms.

CLEA

THE TRAGEDY OF IN

EDITED BY BILL DEVALL

R C U T

DUSTRIAL FORESTRY

SIERRA CLUB BOOKS / EARTH ISLAND PRESS

TABLE OF CONTENTS

Collectively, the photographs in this book provide a portrait of the great forests of North America as they cling to life at the end of the twentieth century. They reveal that the forests of North America are suffering from a massive, human-caused, catastrophic event—an epidemic of massive clearcutting.

Trygve Steen